CW01500878

The Italians

Sergio Néster

Text: Sergio Néster
Illustrator: Natasha Bo. / Editor: Sviatlana Papova
Tech. Specialist: N. Monroe / Layout Designer: Ruslan Nabiev
Language adaptation: Nathan Loy

I live in Italy, among Italians.
And it seems to me that I know these people. On the one hand, I wouldn't want to write an ode to Italians — after all, they are ordinary people. Just like everyone else. With pros and cons.

At the same time, I love Italians endlessly. And personally, for me, they are not the same as everyone else. So, perhaps, expecting objectivity from me is not worth your time. But I hope that these short sketches from the life of Italians can tell you a little bit more about how amazing Italy is and how incredible the people are who live there.

This book is called "The Italians", but it could be called "The Italy". Because Italy is its people.

—

All characters and events are not fictional.
Any resemblance to real people and events is not accidental.

The Italians

—

Contents

Chapter 1

Giacomo & Giuseppe

What do you need to say to get an espresso and half a glass of still water at 8:10 in the morning in the bar across the street? Absolutely nothing. You can just walk in and be as silent as a sea bass. It doesn't matter who's behind the counter: the co-owner of the bar, Giacomo, who wears only a T-shirt in any weather — because the enormous coffee machine, as large as a concert grand piano, instantly heats everything around it. Including Giacomo himself, of course. Giacomo loves to sing, pluck dry twigs from the plants in large terracotta pots on both sides of the bar entrance, and play with with his hair — curly, almost bald, green, purple. That's all Giacomo.

Or Giuseppe, the second co-owner of the bar, resembling a pirate with a beer belly, in a snug striped T-shirt, clearly emphasizing his presence, and a large round earring in his ear. Giuseppe and Giacomo are together, and they are the owners of the bar.

Then there's the cheerful Martina, who works there, always in a cute denim jumpsuit kind of like the character from the Minions movie resembling the pointy-nosed villain.

It doesn't matter who's behind the counter: they all do the same thing. Because they know that I always come at 8:10, right after dropping off the kids at school, and order the same thing: an espresso and still water. I don't even need to say anything.

You walk in, greet them, complain about the weather, praise the weather, joke, ask "how are you?" — and you get asked the same. And there, your espresso lightly clinks against the bar as it's placed on a porcelain saucer. Well, and half a glass of water.

Still water, naturally.

Chapter 2

The Neighbor Below

Twenty years ago, I arrived in Rome for the first time, and it started snowing. A phenomenon Romans hadn't seen in God knows when. As a result, the residents of the Eternal City unanimously agreed on the only plausible explanation for the phenomenon: I brought it with me.

Hopefully, history won't repeat itself because this winter in Perugia (the city where I live), a massive snowfall began—a rarity not seen in 14 years, promptly dubbed "nevicata storica" — historical snowfall, that is.

To describe the situation in the city briefly: excitement, mild panic, and an obvious overreaction in measures for just a light snowfall, such as the complete closure of schools and the immediate shutdown of the local fish market.

In all fairness, my neighbor Pasquale didn't succumb to the elements. Instead of supporting the panicked moods of worried citizens, he built a snowman and a queue immediately formed to take selfies with it.

Pasquale owns a newsstand located right under my balcony. To give you an idea of how close that is: close enough that I don't water my flowers until 7:30 pm. Because if I do it earlier, water flows onto Pasquale's newspapers and magazines. Understanding this problem didn't come right away — I initially attempted to water the flowers earlier. I didn't immediately grasp why Pasquale was rushing around with newspapers, shouting something in Sicilian. Apologies were in order. My neighbor wasn't born in Sicily; his parents were. However, the Sicilian temperament seems to have been successfully passed down to the son.

Pasquale enjoys riding a bicycle. No, not a leisurely bicycle with a wicker basket in front. A real racing bike with tight cycling gear adorned in logos of sports brands unknown to me as a sports amateur. But he only does it once a week.

It's a common belief that Italians are lazy, work little, and are not very energetic. Sometimes it's true. But not always. Pasquale opens the newsstand at 7:00 am and closes it at 7:30 pm. Every day, except Sunday. On Sundays, he goes cycling. Exactly once a week.

Not long ago, Giacomo and Giuseppe (their bar is right across from Pasquale's newsstand) bought a dog and, for some reason, named it Caesar. Undoubtedly, this added charm to our little cozy Italian courtyard. Previously, my neighbor Pasquale used to shout "Buongiorno" to the entire courtyard from early morning. Now, in addition to "Buongiorno", he loudly and emphatically greets Giacomo and Giuseppe's pet with the phrase "Ave, Caesar!"

It's amusing to wake up to the sounds of "Ave, Caesar!" I must admit.

—

Chapter 3

Martina

This morning in the bar — the one right in front of my house — an unusual conversation took place. Well, no — let me start from the beginning.

So, I come to this bar every morning right after dropping off my kids at school. And I pay exactly one euro for my morning espresso. It's been almost a year.

The espresso has always been served to me in a small red cup. There are other cups, white ones, which I've never had the pleasure of trying. I didn't even notice this for a whole year.

But this morning, Martina (the one who wears a denim jumpsuit like a character from the Minions movie and never seems to be sad) leaned towards me and said:

— Listen, I need to tell you something. I'm sorry, but the coffee supplier has raised prices again, darn it, and we just can't afford to pour coffee into red cups for special customers anymore. But you can choose — either in the red cup or the white one. The red ones will be 20 cents more.

And it's kind of not very good news: prices have gone up again, inflation, crisis — what's good about that? But on the other hand, it unexpectedly turned out that for a whole year, unknowingly, I was a special customer of this bar, and they poured a different coffee just for me. Damn, that's nice.

It's not that I didn't believe Martina, but I decided to experiment and try the coffee in the white cup — the one that can still be bought at a reasonable price of just one euro.

And it's not the same. Not at all. If I hadn't been drinking it every morning for a whole year, I might have thought it was just my imagination. But no, it wasn't. Starting tomorrow morning, I'll continue to take it in the red cup — even if it's a bit more expensive.

—

Chapter 4

Francesco

To fit in among Italians, you either need to love football or love food. I'm not a fan of football, but I do love food. Francesco loves food too. He also loves the guitar. More precisely, guitars in general — he has two of them. He carefully keeps them in two large, old cases with soft red fur inside. But it seems that Francesco loves food more than both of his guitars combined.

— How do you make "carbonara"? With "pancetta"? No, no, only with "guanciale"!

— What kind of cheese do you use? "Parmigiano"?! Are you out of your mind! Only "pecorino" and only "romano"!

— And how many eggs do you add? Pff... again, you're doing it all wrong. And so on. As far as I understand, according to his version, the only correct ingredient I have left is water.

Neither of us are chefs, but we both find it interesting to chat about cooking, which we often do. Italy is a perfect place for that — you can discuss cuisine for hours with anyone, whether it's a plastic surgeon or a bus driver.

If you meet someone from a new country you know little about, what would you ask about it? Perhaps you'd inquire about its exact location on the map, the climate, religion, whether anyone managed to build communism or save democracy there, how people feel about Donald Trump, and if they've recently spotted a Yeti. Probably, an Italian would ask too. Probably.

But what he definitely wants to know about a completely unfamiliar country is its "piatto tipico". Which means — «Typical dish». The main dish in your country. That's what he'd want to know. That's what really matters to him to understand what kind of country it is. This is what will tell him much more than the color of your national flag and how people there feel about Trump.

Italians are ready to talk about food anytime, anywhere, with anyone. And it's not about just filling the stomach with anything. On the contrary, Italians savor cuisine, treat it with reverence, attention, and genuine interest. It's not only about the final dish; it's the ingredients that matter: where they come from, how they are grown. And it's crucial that they are Italian.

Recently, I bought walnuts at the market. Very tasty. The bag of walnuts had a casually written inscription in black marker on the cardboard with the price: "Francia". France, that is.

If it had said "Italia" on the cardboard, it would have immediately affected their cost. Because due to that simple word "Italia," the price would have increased by at least twenty percent.

And not because French walnuts are worse. They're, generally speaking, no worse — I bought both, and I didn't notice any difference. Perhaps, there is a difference, and subtle connoisseurs of walnuts will see it. I don't. And you don't. In summary: connoisseurs of walnuts — probably yes; us (almost everyone who buys them) — no.

And it's not always about walnuts. I bought dorado from Greece for €7 and Italian dorado for €15, and now we need to call a fish expert right after the walnut expert to help discern the difference.

Almost any product that has "Italia" written on it automatically becomes more expensive. Or, to be more precise, it's perceived value is higher.

And it's not about the quality of the products — it's about the Italians' attitude toward their country, which I never cease to admire: ours, Italian, is the best — no doubts. Even if you have to pay an extra twenty percent for the idea.

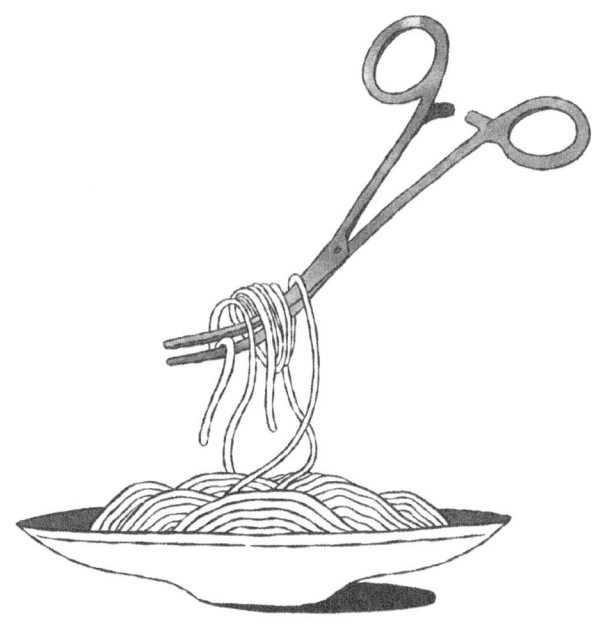

By the way, Francesco is not a bus driver.
He is a plastic surgeon.

—

Chapter 5

Barbara

The house I live in is approximately three hundred years old. Maybe a little more. I don't know if the apartments I rent for sure belonged to Barbara, the retiree from Umbria, all those three hundred years. But it's quite likely. In any case, she grew up here, just like her mother.

When I first moved into my Italian apartment, Barbara kindly ensured me that there were some groceries in the refrigerator. She also made sure that I would inevitably find neatly stacked bills on the kitchen table.

A couple of weeks later, the landlady offered to take me for a walk and try traditional Umbrian sweets. She asked the seller for a pastry the size of a walnut, neatly split it in half. One half for her, the other for me.

Overall, she is a very pleasant woman, although, like many residents of Umbria in Italy, a bit frugal. As you might have already guessed. Barbara doesn't like to throw anything away, so the house is full of with interesting things.

For example, there is a handmade vase with a funny little nose. On its wide flat handle is engraved the family crest with a crown, a six-pointed star, and something resembling a snow shovel. I don't think it's actually a snow shovel, but it's impossible to understand what it is, and it needed an explanation.

Over the Italian travertine fireplace hangs an old mirror on a nail: you can't see anything in it, but it doesn't matter — you have to look at the mirror itself, not at the reflection in it.

And my favorite exhibit — a wide ceramic vase on three animal legs, which still remains a mystery to me to this day. One of the theories were a night pot and a container for heating rooms with coal. There is still no final verdict.

The fireplace doesn't work, and using it for its intended purpose is impossible. But it can accommodate a whole bunch of wax candles, and the travertine shelf has become home to a collection of trinkets.

Once I tried to delicately inquire with Barbara if there was any way to restore the fireplace to working condition. Barbara replied that it could probably be done. At my expense, of course. Despite the not-so-pleasant conditions for repair, I attempted to fix the fireplace. However, I chose the wrong time — about a week before Christmas.

In the end, the chimney sweep I found through the advertisement promised to call me right after the holidays. But, of course, he didn't call. Thus, the travertine fireplace remained just a shelf, and I discovered that in Italy, the official profession of a chimney sweep still exists.

In the same place as the non-functional fireplace, in the living room, there is a small library that I don't use. And I have valid reasons for that. The library consists of numerous albums featuring works of medieval artists, mostly of extremely infernal content. Have you ever seen an image of Saint Lucy? What about Saint Sebastian?

According to the legend, the young Christian Lucy refused to marry a pagan. He reported her to the local ruler, who ordered her to be sent to a brothel. The rebellious Sicilian gouged out her eyes and sent them to her would-be groom. As a result, Saint Lucy started to be depicted with her eyes in her hands. Or on a book. Or on a tray — which looks even more ominous.

Saint Sebastian doesn't look much better — medieval artists portrayed the martyr pierced with arrows, according to church canons. I don't know if the canons specify a certain number of arrows that the medieval painter was obligated to be thrusted into Sebastian, but artists usually didn't skimp on their quantity.

Another saint, whose name I don't remember, was depicted with a cleaver stuck impressively in the head of Christian souls' remarkable size. With a high degree of realism. Often, even too much.

Then there's Saint Agatha — also with a tray, but this time, instead of eyes, it features a female breast, formerly belonging to Agatha, and Saint Stephen, stoned. The saints are interspersed with numerous scenes from hell with monsters, devouring sinners with enviable appetite — how can we do without them? In general, I didn't like the library.

There is also something like an attic in the house. Well, no, it's not an attic because to have one, you would need to live on the top floor. And mine is not the top — it's the first, if we don't count the ground floor. The attic in the house is something like a huge mezzanine. Like a giant wardrobe laid on its side and screwed to the ceiling. With two disproportionately small doors compared to the huge wardrobe, which never close. They probably used to close, but not anymore.

Since this remarkable construction is located right under the ceiling (and the ceilings in Barbara's family apartments are very high), it took me exactly a year to muster the courage to explore its contents.

Before that, the highest I had ascended was only once — when I tried to attach an inflatable Christmas star to a small metal hook on the kitchen ceiling. To pull it off, I had to stack two stools on the kitchen table.

But let's get back to the attic. Inside, old suitcases were found, one of which was filled to the brim with old handmade Christmas decorations, a wooden prosthesis, and a massive supply (a box of ten to twelve) of glass beer mugs featuring emblems of a dozen different brewers. Most commonly among the images were hops cones and buxom waitresses in traditional costumes with beer glasses in both hands. I don't know if my landlady's family had any connection to beer, but I haven't seen such a quantity of beer mugs even in a bar.

Among other things, Barbara's house has a heavy wooden chest. Well, at first, I thought it was a chest. Until I realized that it was not a chest at all, but an old radio. Today, you could pack speakers into it that would be enough for a small Ibiza, but in the past, it was different. Now this wooden block just takes up space, and the only way to use it in any way is to store phone chargers and toothbrushes on the only small shelf it has. That's it — nothing more. Oh yes, also a square white thing that stands on it, emitting WiFi. Now, truly, that's everything.

Although, in all seriousness, I still like it — there's something about it, despite its complete uselessness.

—

Chapter 6

Stefano

About an hour's drive from my home, there is a small Tuscan town called Cortona. Yes, the one where they filmed "Under the Tuscan Sun" about a San Francisco writer who decided to find solace in Tuscany after her divorce and impulsively bought a villa there. That's where I'm heading.

No, I'm not planning to buy a villa — I want to photograph Tuscany and indulge in autumn-roasted chestnuts.

I entered a bar near the train station, ordered a coffee, paid for it at the counter. Another person named Stefano is the one making the coffee. Stefano and I are not acquainted — his name is written with a black marker on a small cardboard badge on his apron.

So, after placing an order, you need to move a bit away from the counter, closer to Stefano and his warm coffee machine, the heat of which can be felt even at a distance of one and a half meters. I am quite pleased with that, by the way — Umbrian mornings in October are not typically warm, and I'm already feeling quite chilly. I enjoy warming myself up, while I wait for my espresso.

The person at the counter says:

— Stefano, did you make coffee for the signore?

— I did.

— Then why didn't you give it to him?

— Who should I give it to?

— Well, give it to the signore.

— Where is he, this Signore?

— Are you blind? There he is, right in front of you — says the cashier, pointing at me.

— Ah, well... Why are you confusing me?! What the hell, Signore? This is ragazzo!

If "signore" is clear without translation, then "ragazzo" in Italian means a young man. Clearly, not reaching the age of "signore".

However, he (meaning me, in this case) does not fall short of being a "signore" only by Italian standards. I am forty-two.

Italians have a unique attitude towards age. I don't think it's possible anywhere else to be a "ragazzo di quaranta due anni" — a young man of forty-two. Who is still considered too young to be called a "signore".

It is believed that in space, time does not flow like on Earth. In Italy, it doesn't flow like anywhere else either. I don't know what conclusion can be drawn from all this, but that's how it is. Italians don't believe that life ends after forty. Or fifty. Or sixty. They travel, run, cook, draw, sing, dance, and use Nordic walking sticks to tap on the cobblestones of medieval Italian towns. By the way, my neighbor Pasquale doesn't seem to like Nordic walking sticks for some unknown reason. He says they're strange. He didn't specify what exactly is strange and what's wrong with Nordic walking sticks.

By the way, the San Francisco writer wasn't 18 either, but her desperate attempt to start a new life in Italy can be considered successful. At least, according to the script.

Chapter 7

Simona

Simona is my "commercialista", which means accountant. A pleasant woman of around 45. Quite young, as we
found out in the previous chapter about the signore who
is too young to be called that.

After my first visit to Simona's office, for some reason,
what stood out the most to me was the cabinet with
documents. Sturdy, intricately carved, with elegant glass
facades and somewhat amusing animal-like feet instead
of legs.

The accountant, like many things in Italy, came to me
through connections. Similarly, by the way, I found the
apartment for rent, a school for the children, and a dentist. In Italy, almost everything is done through word
of mouth. You can, of course, do without them. But it
will be worse, less reliable, and more expensive. The last
point, by the way, does not always hold true. Sometimes,
through word of mouth, things turn out to be not much
cheaper. But the first two can be considered quite opera-
tional.

But just having connections is not enough. Simona has been my accountant for a year and a half, and it took me exactly that long to get her phone number. Before that, the process of contacting the accountant did not look like a simple message on WhatsApp. You had to call the office, introduce yourself, and request a telephone audience with Simona. Don't forget about "pausa pranzo"— the Italian equivalent of the Spanish siesta when lunch extends for about three to four hours. Approximately from 1 to 4 p.m.

Of course, we need to make allowances for the rather strict region of Italy where I live. Umbria considers itself quite closed, but, honestly, everything suits me.

There are two things in Italian Umbria that I unequivocally like: the people and the breathtaking views. The people, perhaps, are a bit less open than in Southern Italy but not as closed as Northerners. Besides, Southern hospitality is good, but if it lasts for a long time, it can be a bit exhausting. Here, it's just right.

So, for about a year, I went to Simona's office to unravel the complexities of my relationship with Italian bureaucracy a bit more and admire the carved cabinet with animal-like feet. And for a whole year, I tried to pay Simona for her services. Every time I brought up the topic of payment, I heard her usual "let's do it later". I don't know if it mattered that I came to Simona through word of mouth, or if it's just the usual style of client relationships, but it was a bit unusual, I must admit.

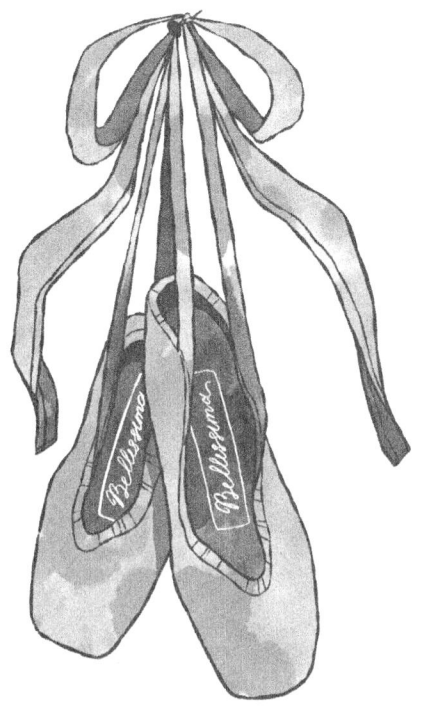

I also don't know if our accidental meeting at the annu-
al dance school concert had anything to do with me finally getting Simona's phone number. Simona, as it turned
out, takes her daughter to the dance school owned by my
acquaintance. The same acquaintance who invited me to
watch the concert. Slightly confusing? That's how it was
supposed to be. After all, we are in Italy.

Chapter 8

Gianluca

"Okay, Google. How to eat a cactus?" Have you ever done that? I have. Once.

I saw cactus fruits at the market and couldn't resist. I was already familiar with their taste — I had bought them before, but already peeled. But trying them whole was a different experience.

Google, I must say, didn't help much because after eating the cacti, I needed tweezers to get rid of the thin, barely noticeable needles that got stuck in my fingers and palms, which later proved to be quite challenging to remove.

But usually, I don't need Google to understand how to eat a cactus, how to prevent chicory from being bitter, or how to cook thistle. By the way, it's not a joke — thistle is indeed prepared in Italy, and here it's called "cardo". The cactus incident happened because this time the vegetable stall seller Gianluca didn't show up, and I had to rely on my own efforts. In vain, as you've already understood.

Gianluca doesn't just sell vegetables. He knows everything about them. When I first came to his stall, I saw a child's drawing. It depicted onions, zucchinis, bunches of lettuce, and potatoes in bags with nets. In the center of the picture was Gianluca himself. Understandably, it's challenging to catch the resemblance, but below there was a caption "papa" — dad. To prevent the drawing from getting wet and to keep it in its original form, Gianluca laminated it. Then he permanently placed the homemade icon in the most prominent place — right in front of the large iron scales. Very charming, I think.

Moreover, it was utterly impossible to walk past flat wooden crates, the bottom of which was lined with brown paper. Chestnuts lay in the crates — chocolate-brown, very appetizing in appearance. I decided to buy them.

"Do you have a pan with holes?" the seller asks.

"No, I'm used to using pans without holes", I try to counter the strange question.

"No, you definitely need a pan with holes — otherwise, how are you going to roast chestnuts?"

And, of course, I don't have one. Moreover, I didn't even know what it looked like.

As a result of my negative answer to the question about the pan, there was a slight pause because Gianluca had already packed the chestnuts into a pleasantly rustling paper bag.

"Okay, don't worry; you can do without the pan. Toss them in the oven, and it'll be fine. Just don't forget to make a cut on them — like a cross — or they'll explode".

Luckily, nothing exploded.

After the chestnuts came chicory, which I had once tried in one of the Umbrian trattorias and firmly decided to reproduce this controversial dish at home. Overall, it turned out well. After following Gianluca's instructions precisely.

After chicory, there was a massive mushroom, the exact name of which I don't remember. Gianluca said they call them "elephant ears" in his hometown in Apulia. I don't know about the similarity to ears, but they are indeed not small. The recipe for pasta with huge mushrooms was immediately given to me after I purchased them. Like every time I bought something from him.

By the way, I found a pan with holes. How to describe it... it's like someone shot a shotgun point-blank into a thin metal pan. Yes, it's hard to describe it more accurately.

I didn't buy it because I didn't plan to roast chestnuts on an industrial scale. But I wanted to see what it looked like.

Chapter 9

The Man in the Coat

With cacti seemingly sorted out, there's another question:

Have you ever been told to go to hell? I have. And sometimes they did it quite gracefully.

When I first arrived in Rome with enthusiasm in my eyes and a student visa in my passport, I managed to get quite absurdly lost right on Piazza Venezia — in the very center of Rome. Google Maps was scarce back then, and instead of an iPhone, I had a Nokia 2110 in my pocket. Grayish-blue, with buttons.

It was early morning, and there were hardly any people on the street. A senior gentleman in a hat and a fine overcoat leisurely strolled past me. He walked slowly down the street, occasionally glancing upwards, either at the roofs of luxurious Roman palazzos or at the deep blue sky.

I greeted the passerby and abruptly rushed towards him. I immediately started waving my hands and, in broken Italian, tried to figure out how the hell I could finally get to Campo de' Fiori or something like that.

The gentleman said nothing. He didn't even look at me — he elegantly waved his hand upward and continued walking. In theory, I should have taken offense. But I didn't.

I understood, or rather, didn't quite understand but felt on some subconscious level, that the seemingly haughty gentleman simply didn't want to be impolite. He just wanted to continue his morning stroll peacefully, with the full right to dissolve into his own thoughts and enjoy the aroma of Roman cafes, without being distracted by anything or anyone.

Including me.

And at that moment, I thought that when I get older, I'll also buy myself a hat and a fine overcoat. Just to resemble this elderly descendant of noble patricians a little — he's just so self-sufficient, darn it.

Almost twenty years have passed since that moment. I haven't become a Roman aristocrat yet, but I did buy myself a hat and a fine overcoat.

—

Chapter 10

Lucia

Lucia works in a small pizzeria right in the heart of the city. Small is an understatement in every sense of the word.

The pizzeria is so tiny that there's no room for a single table inside, so they placed them outside. They are also small. Moreover, they are arranged in a narrow row because there isn't much space outside either. Yes, Italy can be a bit snug in places, that's true. And it's not just about parking spaces.

Here, they sell "pizza al taglio". Large square pizzas that are sliced into pieces and sold by weight. Perhaps, that's why the menu doesn't feature traditional round pizzas — there simply wouldn't be a place to put them. No, of course, that's a joke. I don't think it has anything to do with that.

Most likely, they specialize in "pizza al taglio", and the small square tables outside have nothing to do with the square slices of pizza on display. But it's amusing, isn't it?

So, to get your slice of pizza, you need to squeeze inside, choose your desired flavor, pay the bill — and you can settle at one of the small square tables outside. By the way, choosing your table requires caution: due to being placed on medieval cobblestones, many of them sway in all directions. If you only have pizza, no big deal. If you also have a drink with your pizza — that's a problem.

Identifying problematic tables can be done by looking down — usually, folded napkins are placed under the table legs to somehow address the issue of uneven surfaces. It reduces the problem but doesn't completely solve it. In general, you get the hint.

One might think that when Italians bake pizza, it should be perfect. Yes, it is perfect. But not entirely. When the large square pizza is pulled out of the oven, it turns out that somewhere the hand of the "pizzaiolo" slightly trembled, and the incredibly aromatic "gorgonzola" cheese didn't distribute evenly. Or the edge of the pizza in one spot got a bit more burnt than necessary. Or the salty Italian anchovies gathered on the square sea of dough in a bunch rather than individually. Probably out of habit. In short, when the large square with toppings is cut into pieces, it becomes evident that not all pieces are the same.

And here comes a simple but remarkable thing. It's clear that everyone wants to get the best slice. Everyone who comes to the pizzeria wants to get the best one available. And so do I.

Lucia rings up the bill, hands over the slice of pizza. "This is exactly what I wanted. This is the very best one", you think. Then you come again. And again, you get the very best slice. And again.

It's not about whether it has mushrooms, four cheeses, or my beloved zucchini flowers. It's not about its taste, which, by the way, is quite good but can be better. This slice of pizza is the very best one. Out of the ones available on the counter. And that's what matters.

And even if it doesn't have four cheeses. Three. Two. No cheese at all. Without zucchini flowers. It doesn't matter. What matters is that Lucia will always choose the very best slice for you. And you will always choose this place.

Damn, it's that simple.

—

Chapter 11

Pietro

The first time I saw Pietro was on the day of my move to Umbria. It was quite chilly, and Pietro was walking down the street, dressed in a long dark-green coat almost down to his ankles, with a wooden cross and an icon under his arm. One might not attach much significance to this encounter, but the next day, I saw him again on the same street, in the same long coat, with the cross and icon under his arm. And the day after, and the day after that. In the coat, with the cross and icon.

Pietro used to be a doctor. A good one, they say. One evening, he came home and found his wife with a lover. Who, by the way, happened to be a local priest.

This event was such a blow to the doctor to the extent that he decided to end his life. The suicide attempt was unsuccessful, but it affected Pietro's sanity. He started carrying a wooden cross and an icon everywhere, and, for some reason, sewed the Vatican coat of arms onto his sweater. By hand, with uneven stitches. But the coat of arms has held up for at least two years now.

Pietro began to roam the streets of Perugia, addressing passersby and reminding everyone about the imminent Judgment Day, which was bound to happen any day now. And that if they didn't repent right now, they would burn forever in the Fiery Gehenna. Well, in general, it all looks quite eerie.

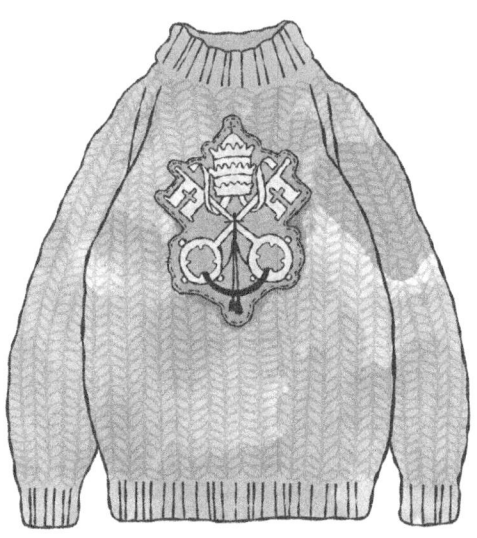

One might think that a former doctor, whom personal tragedy turned him into town madman, was doomed to become an outcast. Who would want to listen day after day to sermons from a self-proclaimed priest in a knitted sweater with the Vatican coat of arms?

But no, Pietro didn't become an outcast. Neighbors didn't shun him, people didn't stop greeting him back, and they didn't show annoyance in response to his sermons. People on the street treat the doctor, who has survived his mind, completely normally; they don't question the existence of the Fiery Gehenna and offer him cigarettes, which Pietro doesn't buy himself. Either it's a sin or he's saving money. I'm not sure.

And it's not just Pietro. Recently, I went to the supermarket, and while waiting in line at the checkout, I observed a political dispute between a supermarket employee and a local "barbone" — a homeless person. By the way, if not for the dispute, the line would have moved much faster. But this is Italy; that's how things are here. I got used to it a long time ago, so I patiently waited for the end of the heated discussion, practicing reading texts in Italian on cans of peas.

Sure, the supermarket employee is not a senator or an honorary member of Parliament. But socially, there's still a huge gap between them. Actually, not just a gap — it's a chasm. But it was absolutely unfelt. I didn't hear any hint of disrespect from the supermarket employee towards his interlocutor. Nothing that would say, "Hey, who do you think you are? What does your opinion matter? Have you seen yourself in the mirror?"

Nothing of the sort. Just a political discussion between two people with the same passports. And it didn't matter whether he had a home and what he was dressed in.

—

Chapter 12

Sandro

I was 22, studying in Rome, and working as a "cameriere" — a waiter in a restaurant owned by an older Italian named Sandro, who was born and raised in Rome. Something that can now be considered a rarity.

The pay at the restaurant was modest, but it covered my food and evening beers. Additionally, I had free accommodation in an extension of the restaurant, decent tips, and the opportunity to observe Italian life from the inside. That was quite good.

Sandro was a pleasant elderly Italian with a questionable past and a large black Jaguar, which was parked in the garage of the same place where I lived.

No, I didn't live in the garage. It was a big place divided into several rooms.

In one of them, they stored equipment for the restaurant — an antique coffee machine of gigantic size, some dishes, and a bright red contraption for slicing "prosciutto" into thin, almost transparent slices — as they like to do in Italy. I don't know if this machine could still slice anything thinly, considering it looked like it was a hundred years old. But it managed to preserve its charismatic bright red color despite the rust.

In the second room was my living space. There was no heating since officially the place wasn't considered a dwelling. Despite that, a regular electric heater easily coped with the mild Roman winters. In general, it wasn't cold. It was noisy. All because the roof consisted of metal sheets. And nothing else. So, whenever it rained, the roof turned into a large drum, making it utterly impossible to fall asleep to its accompaniment. That was probably the only downside.

On a positive note, there was a tall peach tree right in front of the entrance. From it, you could survey the Roman hills while enjoying incredibly aromatic peaches.

And the third room was the garage, where Sandro's Jaguar languished in confinement. The owner would open the garage, remove the tight black cover, and gently caress it over the black hood. Then, he would run his fingers over the predator emblem, attached a bit higher than the chrome radiator grille. And that's it. After another meeting with his pet, he would carefully wrap the car in its cover, and an unpleasant moment of parting for Sandro would ensue.

The Jaguar couldn't leave the garage because it was purchased with money not declared on Sandro's tax return. It's hard to say exactly how these funds were obtained, but the Italian "Guardia di finanza" would certainly disapprove of this method.

—

Chapter 13

Paolo

Despite the garage with Sandro's illegal pet being on the restaurant premises, he didn't pay much attention to it. A couple of years ago, he leased the restaurant to Paolo, who was doing his best to make ends meet.

"Paolo, ma basta, ti prego! Non si può respirare qui dentro!" (Paolo, enough, please! It's impossible to breathe in here!)

Paolo's wife once again unsuccessfully pleaded with her husband to stop using vinegar to clean cutlery and switch to something more progressive. Paolo had no intention of admitting defeat to progress and continued to add vinegar to a large bowl with knives and forks bathing in it. After which, he meticulously wiped them with a soft cloth. And indeed, they sparkled, it must be acknowledged.

The persistent smell of vinegar wafted through the establishment, and there was no chance it would dissipate by the time the restaurant opened. But none of the patrons ever complained.

Despite having a reasonably good kitchen, the restaurant was not doing well. The first thing Paolo did was change the name. But that proved insufficient. Business still went poorly.

Paolo often argued with his wife, not only about the need to use vinegar but also about the principles of managing the restaurant. At the same time, he had to take her opinion into account because, in Italy, any business almost automatically becomes a family affair.

Paolo also had to consider the opinion of his not-so-young mother, who also participated in the life of the family restaurant and invariably wore a "bob" hairstyle. Every evening, she sat at a small table near the entrance, smiling at visitors and handing out bills. Frankly, she was quite an unpleasant signora. I didn't like her, and she didn't like me either.

Paolo's sister married Valentino, who came from Romania and became the restaurant manager. After that, almost the entire staff of the restaurant quickly became Romanian. Everyone: chefs, waiters, even the woman who washed the dishes and the parking attendant who didn't speak a word of Italian.

To be fair, he didn't need to. He had a stick with a red circle on it, with which he pointed customers to the parking spots. Yet, he didn't want to part with the stick even when there was no one to park. In that case, he twirled it on his hand by the string, tracing neat figure eights in the air.

The only non-Romanian was the "pizzaiolo" — the chef specialized exclusively in pizza. He was Sicilian and consistently used strange curses that I never heard from anyone else.

The head chef in Paolo's restaurant was a woman. From Romania, as you might have guessed. Usually, chefs in Italy are men, but there are always exceptions. It's hard to say how good of a chef she was, but some aspects of her approach to work displeased the patrons.

For instance, when she made "risotto", she would dip her finger directly into the dish sharply, so as not to burn herself, taste the finger, and continue working. Being confident that there was just the right amount of salt, and the sauce was not too sour and thick enough. One day, a client witnessed this and caused a grand scandal. Paolo struggled to pacify the client — he had to lie, saying it was risotto for the staff.

By the way, in reality, Paolo treated his staff very respectfully and didn't make any distinctions between risotto for the staff and risotto for the clients.

Despite having clear problems in the restaurant business, many of Paolo's principles were, at the very least, respectable. I usually worked three days a week — on Friday, Saturday, and Sunday. Every Sunday, after closing the restaurant, Paolo paid me for three days of work. And each time, he said, "thank you". Yes, getting paid for work is important, and it seems quite enough.

But when you spend three days running with plates between tables and at the end of each of them, haul
a couple of heavy black garbage bags to the bins located about three hundred meters from the restaurant, the
word "thank you" is certainly not superfluous.

Every time, without exception, on Sunday evenings,
along with the cash, I received Paolo's customary
"thank you".

Nice? Damn right.

Chapter 14

Slightly Nervous Italian

Here in Italy, there's a concept known as "posto fisso".

It's a type of employment where the employee works not on a contract, which may expire sooner or later, but rather has permanent employment. So permanent that it's practically impossible to fire an employee with "posto fisso". Otherwise, Italian unions will simply tear the employer apart. In general, in this world, nothing is more unshakable than the Colosseum and "posto fisso".

One of the places where an Italian can secure the coveted "posto fisso" is the Italian post office. And it's precisely here, at the post office, that one needs to come to request an Italian residence permit. The post office then sends the completed documents to the immigration department of the police.

You arrive, take a paper ticket at the entrance terminal, wait for the number corresponding to your ticket to light up on the display, approach the window, and they hand you an envelope with forms to fill out. You fill them out and return them. The procedure is roughly like that.

So, I came, took a number and in line ahead of me was a Turkish guy who doesn't know any Italian at all. Not a word. Meanwhile, all the forms that need to be filled out are in excellent Italian stationery.

At the window, the Turkish guy was is greeted by a postal employee — a slightly nervous Italian whose name is unknown to me. Let's just call him "Slightly Nervous Italian".

The first attempt to communicate with "Slightly Nervous Italian" ends in a complete failure. The postal worker has no intention of switching to English. He doesn't even consider switching to a simplified version of Dante's language. Although at some point, it seemed to me that Dante himself spoke Italian more simply.

The Turk tries again. In very basic English, probably because he began to realize that the language of Shakespeare is not very familiar to a Dante native speaker. The next attempt by the Turk to breach the impregnable bastion with a glass window turned out to be even worse than the two previous ones. But no one expected such an outcome.

"Slightly Nervous Italian", also the holder of "posto fisso", clearly, articulately, and with expression, uttered the following:

— Siccome tu non parli l'italiano vaffanculo.

Which literally means: "Since you don't speak Italian, go to hell".

End of quote.

Italians not working in banks, government offices, or the Italian post office believe that "posto fisso" should be abolished. I might agree with them.

—

Chapter 15

Alberto

I have a mandolin named Matilda. Until recently, the Neapolitan beauty Matilda boasted eight strings. That was until I accidentally broke one of them. Now there are only seven.

I could, of course, order new strings on Amazon, and I might have done just that. But there's one "but". I don't know how to install them. So, I decided to go to a music store, overpay a bit for the strings, and in return, ask the seller to fix Matilda.

Before the visit, just in case, I called the store and asked if they could save my Neapolitan passion. It took a long time to get through, but eventually, someone on the other end of the line said "okay", Matilda and I immediately set off for the long-awaited meeting with the store owner, Alberto.

We arrived and looked around. I'm not a musician, but I enjoy the sensations of visiting music stores: new guitars shine with yellow lacquered sides, curved chromed pipes on the walls, reflecting visitors amusingly, and next to the cashier stands a large flat box with picks. Pure pleasure.

I extracted Matilda from its case to introduce her to Alberto, the store owner, who is also the cashier, cleaner, loader, and security all in one person. This is not uncommon in Italy, by the way. The format of a small store where the owner performs all other functions is a very Italian story

Owners of small family stores complain about high taxes and try not to hire anyone if possible. In addition, according to Italian law, the employee is always right, not the employer.

Add to all this the Italian trade unions with their quite active position, and it becomes finally clear why Alberto is not only the store owner but also the cashier, cleaner, loader, and so on down the list.

Alberto twirled the mandolin in his hands, placed two square paper envelopes on the table, which he clearly prepared in advance.

— Look, there are two options. The strings are almost identical, just a slight difference in color. This reddish one is copper, and this yellowish one is brass.

And here I suddenly begin to understand that from a small overpayment for the strings, I get an unexpected bonus. The strings in both envelopes, which seem identical, are not entirely the same. The shade is indeed slightly different. I pondered a bit, twisted both envelopes in my hands, chose copper. Slightly more reddish. So subtle that it's physically impossible to discern this difference on the internet.

While I savor the unexpectedly fallen charm of the analog world, Alberto, as if reading my thoughts, says:

— Well, see? They are different shades. How could you have chosen it on the internet?

I immediately begin to understand what we are going to talk about now. We will call Amazon the Universal Evil.

And so it happened. Alberto complained that now music stores in Italy are run exclusively by enthusiasts, it has become difficult to make any profit due to internet giants, and the soul has left music stores.

In general, such conversations are now happening frequently in Italy. Owners of other stores, not just music ones, say roughly the same. And sometimes they also mention the soul.

I don't know, maybe the soul really left.

—

Chapter 16

The Man from the Red Box

Perhaps the title sounds a bit peculiar, and the red box surely has a more conventional name, but it remains unknown to me. Such a box is installed next to the turnstiles at every metro station.

The purpose of the box is simple: it serves to contact metro staff to resolve any issues. To report these problems, one needs to press the button and retell the essence of the problem into the red box.

To exit the metro, you must insert your ticket into the narrow slot of the turnstile. After that, if everything is proceeding as usual, the turnstile will briefly chew on the paper ticket, spit it back out, and, in return, open the doors for your exit.

I inserted the ticket. The turnstile chewed it up. Silence. Nothing.

At that moment, I faced two problems that needed to be addressed to the red box:

1) To exit the metro, the turnstile must open and allow me to do so.

2) I need to retrieve my ticket. Tickets can be for one ride or ten. Mine was for ten. The irony of fate in action.

I press the button, and a cheerful voice of a middle-aged man greets me from the red box. I explain the essence of the problem and wait.

What happens next is more interesting: the voice from the box suggests I take a ride a few stops forward to the terminal station and find a small iron door to the left of the stairs. An engaging quest. I remind you, all this is required just to exit the metro and get back my own ticket.

Suddenly, I catch myself thinking that I am not angry at all. Although there seems to be reason for it: you have to go somewhere far and search for something just to exit the metro and retrieve your own ticket. But no, I am not angry. I am as calm as Mahatma Gandhi. The absurd conditions for ticket return cease to be dreadful, and what is happening inexplicably turns into a light adventure.

By the way, the person behind the small iron door turned out to be a pleasant, gray-haired Italian who handed me 13 euros in cash as a refund for the ticket and apologized profusely for not being able to let me in-to the room. Just in case, he pointed several times to the door, where, in big black letters, it said that entry is only for metro personnel. Not that I really wanted to get in-side, but it was nice.

I think there is some inexplicable magic in the Italians. They organize everything poorly, and any of the possi-ble problems will be solved in the most inefficient way, but you will remain satisfied.

How? Hell knows. But it works. Magic.

—

Chapter 17

Luca

Luca is not a character from a Pixar cartoon. Although expressions like "Santa Mozzarella" or "Santa Gorgonzola" in his performance, I can easily imagine. He doesn't transform into a sea dragon, but he handles dough and cheese with incredible skill. Luca makes pizza.

Every Friday, I go to the pizzeria. The one where the "pizzaiolo" Luca works. Or rather, I go to visit Luca in the pizzeria where he works. Because if he didn't work there, I would probably spend my Friday evenings differently.

The pizzeria has two halls: the first one is small, next to the hot oven and Luca's workspace, and the second one is more spacious and quiet. I always choose a table in the first, small one.

Let it be cramped and noisy, and sometimes it even turns into something like a very loud Irish bar. Because only from this hall can you observe how Luca, with incredible love, stretches balls of dough with his fingers and magically turns them into round, thin cakes. Only from there can you see how Luca spirally spreads Italian tomato sauce on the cake, and then, unexpectedly quickly, throws a handful of grated mozzarella on it. A rare pleasure, I must admit.

Although our relationship with Luca did not begin with rare pleasures. I would even say the opposite.

When I came here for the first time, I discovered in the pizzeria menu a dish unknown to me until that moment: "Pizza Salsiccia e Friarielli". In the description, there was a note with an asterisk: "*stagionale, disponibile in inverno" — a seasonal product, available only in winter.

In general, the temptation was completely and absolutely irresistible.

I don't think dark green leaves resembling algae would provoke the desire in everyone to immediately deal with them with a knife and fork. Or perhaps even barbarically consume all this with bare hands. But for some reason, I did.

Winter had already ended by that time, but I decided to take a risk and asked the waiter if I could somehow still get these wonderful "Friarielli". The waiter went for a consultation with the chef and returned to me after a couple of minutes with a positive answer.

The dish was brought. I tried it. I tried it again.

I understand that describing tastes with text is an ungrateful task. It's like trying to describe "Mona Lisa" by Da Vinci with letters: "Well … what's in the painting … a woman in the painting, she sits on a chair, she's smiling. And there's a landscape behind her, with mountains".

But I will try. Especially since the masterpiece "Friarielli" did not seem to me — what am I risking, after all?

So, take something green, endow it with the scent of stewed cabbage and the taste of broccoli, and generously sprinkle it all with pepper — but in a way as if the lid suddenly fell off the pepper shaker.

Got it? Congratulations, you have tasted "Friarielli". Maybe, unnecessarily. Just like me.

Yes, our love affair with "Friarielli" did not happen. That's life, it happens. But the rest — mmm… No, this time I won't try to describe with text the taste of hot mozzarella and the slight crunch of the dough that has just left the wood-fired oven.

When I leave, I always wave goodbye and shout to the whole pizzeria, "Bravo, maestro!" to express once again my appreciation to the master for another culinary masterpiece. In response, he theatrically puts his flour-covered hand to his heart and bows lightly to me.

Maybe that's why I go to him every week — not just to eat pizza. Although pizza is good, damn it.

P.S. Several months after writing this chapter, I decided to show generosity and give Italian "Friarielli" another chance. Unexpectedly, this time they turned out to be quite good. I'll have to rehabilitate the reputation of my dark green friends and admit that the accusations against them were completely undeserved.

—

Chapter 18

Giovanni

— Pronto! Yes, yes, Signor Notary, we are not far, we will arrive soon. My real estate agent, Giovanni, hung up and looked at me:

— Coffee?

And when did I ever refuse coffee? Of course, I'll have coffee. Yes, I understand that Giovanni and I are running late for my own deal to buy an Italian apartment. But it's coffee.

So, 10:12 am, we leisurely drink strong espresso, and our deal was supposed to start 12 minutes ago, exactly at 10:00 am.

— Pronto! Yes, Signor Notary, we are on our way. There are roadworks here, terrible traffic jams. Yes, yes, I know it was supposed to start at 10:00, we'll be there soon. Yes, yes, we will definitely be there, a presto!

You know, there are things that seem amazing only because you don't know how to do them.

Like a basketball player throwing a heavy rubber ball across half the court, and it miraculously lands right in the metal ring. How the hell? How does he do that?

So, how does Giovanni do it? How does he lie so smoothly? If I hadn't been having coffee with him right now, I wouldn't have doubted for a second that there was a completely unpredictable transportation collapse. And solely for this reason, we arrived at 10:46, not exactly at 10:00 am.

To be fair, it should be said that the notary, the only one of the three parties, arrived on time. The seller of the apartment also arrived with a significant delay. Probably, traffic jams too.

The notary approached the matter very seriously: he read out loud absolutely everything, down to every letter, in the purchase agreement. Despite the fact that it's a tiny apartment of only 26 square meters.

All right, now I am the happy owner of an Italian apartment. However, there is a catch.

Currently, my apartment is inhabited by a Moroccan man whom I haven't even seen. He has a lease agreement that he made with the previous owner of the apartment, allowing him not to open the door for me for another year and a half. But according to Giovanni, he is about to move out. Do you understand, right? The thing is, I understand. And I understood it even before the purchase.

Of course, you may have a reasonable question: then why did I need it? The thing is, problems are not only with the apartments that Giovanni sold me.

Buying an apartment in Italy turned out to be an invaluable life experience.

Now I can confidently say that I've seen it all.

I saw a ghost apartment without any documents — they couldn't even find them in the local commune. That is, they just don't exist. At all.

I saw apartments with a sofa, kitchen, and washing machine that, according to documents, are a warehouse, so legal residence there is not possible.

I saw an apartment where somehow more than 10 citizens of Ecuador managed to fit into 30 square meters.

I even saw an apartment with a cave and a trough for horses. Seriously. This place used to be a monastery for Benedictine monks, as proudly informed by the not-so-young owner. The cave was used to store wine bottles. Several bottles, by the way, are still there.

Quite obviously, against this backdrop, the option that Giovanni sold me didn't seem so outrageous. Even though my agent shamelessly lied to me. And I know it. Moreover, it seems to me that he knows it too. It's like a game that must be played: Giovanni pretends to tell the truth, and you pretend to believe it.

Honestly, I even find it interesting to play this game. Even though, according to the strange rules of this game, the role of the loser initially belongs to me.

Chapter 19

The Fish Seller at the Market

There are people who always joke. So much so that you stop understanding when they're joking and when they're serious. The fish seller, from whom I always buy seafood, is one of those people.

No, perhaps "seafood" is not the right word. It doesn't convey the richness and variety of mussels, shrimp, squid, octopus, and other fishy and sea-salty inhabitants of the Mediterranean Sea brought from the sea town of Ancona. Well, never mind that for now.

I come to the market. As usual, on Wednesdays. Next to the stall where they sell eggplants and artichokes from Apulia and hand-painted plates from the neighboring village of Deruta, I scan for a white van.

It's somewhat rusty, weathered by time, not pampered with regular repairs and Italian roads. The seller is the same — worn out over the years of handling heavy plastic crates and burdened by the excessively high Italian taxes. But he tries to keep cheerful and doesn't show it.

Like the van, loaded to the top with marine delicacies. Both are holding up well.

I'm almost familiar with the seller, who skillfully navigates between ice-filled trays. Not knowing each others names, only our faces. The seller waves to me when I'm about fifteen meters away from his van, and I always give praise for the fish that I bought the previous week.

I go for fish once a week, so it turns out to be precisely a week since my last purchase.

Every Wednesday, we exchange the same pleasantries: I praise his goods, and he praises my Italian, which, according to him, is almost accent-free. Not true, but it's nice to hear.

— So, what did you catch today? — I ask my lively seller.

— Oh, and I was just waiting for you! Look what I have: barracuda!

I had seen barracuda in pictures and on TV. In my childhood, I watched Jacques Cousteau diving into the abyss with aqualung, demonstrating the underwater world to the enthusiastic viewers. So, in that underwater world, "barracuda" was a silvery torpedo about a meter and a half long with crocodile-like teeth, not these puny fish with an extremely athletic build on the counter. It still has teeth, though. Small ones.

Upon my exclamation, "Come on, what kind of barracuda is this, damn it!" the seller nodded affirmatively once again and added that if I didn't buy it right away, it would be gone — they would snatch it out of his hands. I bought it, what else could I do? Now I'll be thinking about carrying barracuda home.

In addition to barracuda, I bought "cozze" — mussels. Usually, I bought Sardinian ones in the supermarket, but these, from the neighboring marine region (we don't have a sea), I bought here, from the fish van.

I paid about twice as much as usual — almost ten euros instead of five or six, but they turned out to be really good. Not twice as good as their price, but definitely better than the others from the supermarket. Everything is fine except for one thing: to cook them, you need a free evening — preferably the whole evening, as you have to clean them manually with a metal sponge, one by one. It's fascinating but very, very time-consuming.

In the supermarket, there is a thing that resembles a giant pressure cooker. The seller usually throws the "cozze" you bought into it. After that, the infernal machine starts buzzing and making strange sounds, but in return, it gives you almost clean mussels. Almost, because you still have to clean them manually after that, but it's still easier.

I also need something less exotic than barracuda. I study the trays with ice, carefully look into the eyes of the fish, and try to see tonight's dinner in them.

Understanding my inner turmoil, my almost-familiar fish seller beckons me closer with a sly gesture: "Just recently, Signora took this fish — "cefalo". Said it's "buonissimo". Take this fish — it's good, don't look at the low price".

"Cefalo" turned out to be a beautiful fish with shiny scales of a pinkish-silvery shade. I don't remember exactly how much it cost per kilogram, but one fish cost me only three euros. Even a little less — two euros and eighty cents. Something like that.

I said goodbye to the fish seller until next Wednesday, and the purchases moved to my kitchen. It's not far — about ten minutes, no more. Another half an hour, and the beauty "cefalo" gracefully settled on a pillow made of thin slices of potatoes.

All right, now it's time to put it in the oven. Twenty minutes should be enough, I think.

—

Chapter 20

Luigi

In my parents' living room, there was a large rug. It had the color of ripe cherries, generously adorned with patterns in an Eastern style. It always seemed old-fashioned to me, and as soon as I started living on my own, the first thing I did was buy a rug from IKEA. Solid beige, without a single pattern. It became a perfect addition to the kitchen with glossy white facades and stylish glasses made of transparent glass. Two sizes — large glasses for wine, smaller ones — for water. Exactly six of each. And small shot glasses for liqueur. Also six of them.

In Luigi's trattoria, owned by a former sailor who retired about ten years ago, everything is different. If a careless visitor accidentally knocks over a glass brimming with "vino da casa" — house wine, and shatters it, no one will be looking for the perfect match to the remaining orphaned glasses. It will simply be replaced with a new one. Or an old one, but a different one. In short, with any that can be found.

The tables here come in all kinds, many of which are only nominally tables. One of them is easily recognizable as a wine barrel with a hole for a cork on its bulging side, and a couple of others are large wooden spools, which used to have electric wires wound around them. Before they became tables.

Different chairs accompany the tables — whatever is available will do. The tables are covered with assorted tablecloths, among which you won't find two identical ones, and the cutlery is, of course, from completely different sets.

You might think that the place is deserted. But it's not. On the contrary — if you don't come a little early for lunch or dinner, there won't be a single free table left. Not one made from a wine barrel, nor one made from an electric wire spool. None.

Despite Luigi's maritime past, the sea from his trattoria is quite far away by Italian standards. Twelve kilometers, it seems. Yes, far away. By Italian standards, as I've already mentioned.

So, as surprisingly as it may sound, there is no fish on Sailor Luigi's menu. There is meat, vegetables, and wine. Although, to be fair, there is no actual menu in the trattoria. You just come in and ask what's for lunch today.

Luigi announces a short list of a couple of dishes, each accompanied by an incredibly tasty description. Always using adjectives like "freshest", "crispiest", "tenderest", and "homemade". You want to order everything.

Fortunately, you can pay the bill with a card. Times have changed — cards in Italy are now accepted almost everywhere, and people no longer look at you like an idiot if you don't have cash in your pocket. However, there is no traditional hardcover checkbook.

There's a half-sheet of graph paper torn from a notebook. Luigi attaches an old metal cookie box to the notebook and abruptly pulls on the sheet to tear it roughly in half. That's it, the check is ready.

The amount to pay is written on it with a ballpoint pen. One digit and that's all.

And absolutely no polished design, molecular gastronomy, or identical sets of exactly 6 glasses.

—

Chapter 21

Gabriella

Next to my house, there is a small supermarket. It's summer, and the store's door is wide open. I stand at the checkout and unload my purchases, which, by the way, are not that many — tuna in small cans and a crispy ciabatta. Everything else to make a wonderful salad is already at home.

The woman behind the cash register suddenly jumps up and shouts through the open door:

— Hey, hey, hey! You can't park here! Read what's written on the sign: "no parking!" And don't pretend you don't hear me!

I don't know how one could pretend not to hear, considering the cashier's remarkable vocal abilities. But apparently, someone tried. The cashier's name is Gabriella.

After Gabriella successfully repelled the attack of those eager to park in the wrong place, she felt the need to explain herself. For some reason, to me, not to the person attempting to park.

— See how little space there is here? What am I going to do when they deliver goods? How am I supposed to unload the boxes here? Well, tell me, how?!

And I don't know how. And I still don't know why I should know. Although I can understand Gabriella's anger in general, I once again rejoiced that I don't have a car.

Although I had a car some time ago. But now I'm a pedestrian. Because transporting my iron horse with a German passport to Italy turned out to be expensive and absolutely made no sense. In addition, dealing with insurance, documents, and other bureaucratic "joys" was not in my plans at all.

So, I repeat — I'm a pedestrian. And, for now, I don't regret it at all, rather the opposite. Because parking problems in Italy exist, and they are significant. They affect not only those who planned to deprive Gabriella of the opportunity to unload mozzarella and boxes of red wine. They affect everyone who owns a car.

Earlier, I thought these problems were characteristic only of old Italian cities, where, for understandable reasons, it's impossible to reconstruct anything. But over time, I began to notice that even in the newer parts of the city, they are not much less. I don't know why. Perhaps it's due to the famous Italian ability to organize any process as inefficiently as possible. Including parking, of course.

Or there might be some other explanation, but it's unknown to me. I think most Italians don't know it either.

Meanwhile, owning a personal car in Italy is almost the norm, especially considering the unreliability of public transportation. I don't know, maybe I'll give in later, but for now, it's good like this.

And what I incredibly like is Italians' attitude towards cars — no century-long loans for buying the latest model with a million horsepower engine, no boring care for the iron lady by polishing her sides with a soft cloth. Nothing like that — just a car: whatever you can afford, that's what you buy. You get in, start it, and drive. I definitely like it.

—

Chapter 22

Two Guys with a Jackhammer

Not far from my house, there's a bar I sometimes visit. I came in, ordered a cup of espresso, and peacefully parked it on the table near the entrance. It's the end of August, and sitting inside is the last thing I want to do. Although I've noticed that many Italians do it for entirely unclear reasons. But not me.

Yes, technically, an espresso cup is 30 milliliters of hot water pushed through ground coffee under 15 bars of pressure. All right. Technically.

But for me, all of Italy, and half of humanity, an espresso cup is not just a dry set of technical parameters. It's a ritual. And for any ritual, the right atmosphere is needed.

If it were, for example, a ritual of initiation into the members of a powerful Catholic order, the lights would be dimmed, large wax candles would be lit, and perhaps something sublime would be played on a huge church organ (it's as tall as a two-story mansion).

If it were a bachelor party on the eve of a wedding, there would undoubtedly be no shortage of strong alcohol, and around, long-legged blondes with a bust size of fourth and above would be maneuvering. That's what this ritual demands.

And certainly, members of the Catholic order wouldn't expect half-dressed blondes with a bottle of tequila under their arm, and the last thing bachelor party guests want is musical accompaniment in the form of an organ (even one as tall as a two-story mansion).

On that morning, I wasn't expecting either an organ, blondes, or two guys with a jackhammer. But they came.

Italian cities have problems with traffic organization, and it's clear why. When they built the street where the table with my espresso stands, nobody thought about any traffic. Two horse-drawn carts per hour don't count.

As the situation changed over time, two guys with a jackhammer were sent by the local municipality to make changes to the existing life of the Italian town. And they decided to make these changes by restricting entry to the city center, screwing three cast-iron columns into the roadway.

So, I'm sitting at the table, and drama unfolds a meter and a half away from me involving a jackhammer. Have you ever heard how a jackhammer works? Even if you haven't heard this name, let me explain: it's a massive drill with functions of a demolition hammer.

One of the two Italians is busy with the jackhammer, and the other clearly understands the sad fate of my coffee ritual. And we decided to discuss it. Under the sound of the working jackhammer, of course.

He looked at the cup. Then he looked at me. He nodded towards the central square, where this small street leads, to convey the absolute necessity of installing three cast-iron columns to me. He shrugged, meaning that he can't do anything to save my coffee ritual. Just in case, he pointed to his colleague with the jackhammer. Apparently, to shift at least part of the responsibility for the disrupted ritual. I nodded to demonstrate a lack of complaints and full understanding on my part.

Nobody said a word during all this.

—

Chapter 23

Luciano

If you live in Italy, there are three essential people you need: a family doctor, an accountant, and a good hairdresser. My hairdresser's name is Luciano.

So, the other day, I went to get a haircut. It's an old Italian barbershop, and my "parrucchiere" Luciano is not exactly young anymore. But I like it. The first time, I felt a slight fear realizing that a considerably elderly "signore" might accidentally cut my throat with a dangerous razor, but then I got used to it.

Luciano has a daughter and two dogs. Both dogs appeared in the hairdresser's house at his daughter's request, and she promised to walk them every morning. As often happens, they only experienced mornings together exactly four times.

So now, my hairdresser has to wake up 20 minutes earlier to walk the dogs by himself. Luciano has expressed his regrets about this to me and the other visitors of his small barbershop several times, but he has never mentioned it to his daughter. Luciano's wife passed away when their daughter was 10 years old, and now she's 30. But he still spoils her.

So, I came, comfortably settled into the old barber chair covered with brown leather. Meanwhile, Luciano, carefully wrapped me in a funny cape — so that everything would be even, nothing protruding, and nothing pressing on the client's neck, pampered with cashmere turtlenecks.

I hadn't spent five minutes in the cozy chair when a guy walked into the barbershop who least resembled a potential client. Because he was entirely bald. And, I remind you, we're in a barbershop.

Luciano immediately reached into the pocket of his old-fashioned woolen trousers, took out a 1 euro coin, and neatly placed it in the guy's palm. The new coin owner thanked the hairdresser with a short "grazie" and promptly left.

When I last got a haircut from Luciano, he did the same, but not right away. First, a guy came in, the hairdresser carefully looked at him and shook his head negatively. And then, about twenty minutes later, another guy came in and immediately received a coin from Luciano, which was already prepared — in the pocket of those same old-fashioned trousers.

It was a bit awkward to ask, but my innate curiosity took over:

— Tell me, why did you give a coin to this guy but not to the other one who came in recently?

— Because the first one has been coming for a long time and has clearly chosen this way of living for himself — he's not going to change anything. While the second one might be going through temporary difficulties, and he just needs help getting through this tough period.

At that moment, I understood that this was the answer to my question — the one I still couldn't confidently answer myself: whether to give money to people on the street or not. It's like wanting to live right and help people when you can. At the same time, you realize that good intentions don't always genuinely help and often make things worse.

My hairdresser, with a coin always in his left pocket for someone who truly needs it, found the right answer.

At least, that's how it seems to me.

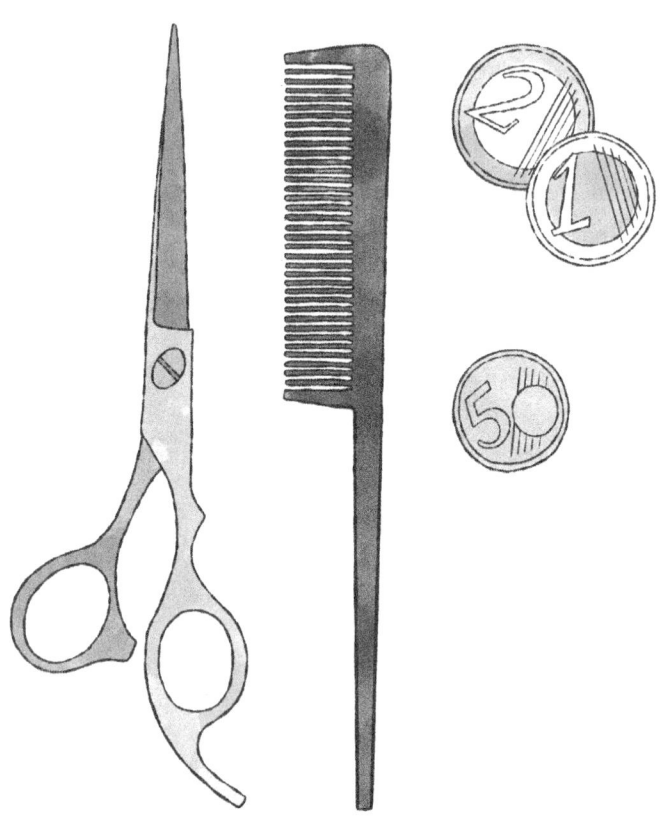

—

Chapter 24

Romolo

The sacred duty of anyone who comes to Rome is to peek through the hole in the roof of the Pantheon and toss a coin into the Trevi Fountain. But that's a story for another time.

Today, I'm in the Monte Sacro district. Here, there is neither the Pantheon nor the Colosseum. It's an ordinary Roman neighborhood away from the center, where ordinary Romans live. Not everyone is fortunate enough to be descendants of noble patricians, and not everyone got apartments next to architectural masterpieces. In this neighborhood, there's a small restaurant owned by Romolo. It opened twenty years ago.

The restaurant owner was born and raised in Rome, and he takes great pride in it. Like most Romans, in fact. Romolo proudly carries the name of one of the two brothers who founded the city where he has spent his entire life.

Romolo was not nurtured by the Capitoline she-wolf, but rather by his mother, Maria. She, moreover, was not a native Roman — she moved to Rome from Naples when she was 17. Romolo's father was also a Neapolitan and worked in his uncle's restaurant, who, in turn, had also moved from Naples. But much earlier. The uncle left the restaurant to Romolo's father, and his father passed it on to his son through inheritance — along with a love for football.

Since Romolo grew up in Rome, he cheers for the "Roma" football club and recognizes no other religions. By the way, in Naples, I saw an icon with the image of the legendary "Napoli" club striker Diego Maradona. So, the comparison with religion is not so random.

The walls, where there is literally not a centimeter of free space, carefully preserve old photos where the owner of the establishment cheerfully smiles at visitors, looking thirty years younger.

In addition to photographs of the smiling Romolo, the walls of the restaurant are scattered with newspaper clippings featuring Francesco Totti (the captain of the "Roma" club) and his autographs. For many, he has become as much a symbol of Rome as the Colosseum. Totti even received the nickname Imperatore di Roma — Emperor of Rome — from grateful city dwellers. Although, in my opinion, that's a bit much.

From time to time, space on the wall is managed by paintings from unknown authors. The plots are incredibly diverse: from half-naked nymphs and portraits of unknown political figures to a fairly realistic scene of the sacking of Rome by barbarians. In addition to epic and not-so-great canvases, a large fish made of iron wire is placed on the wall. Whether the size of the fish exceeded all expectations or there was so little space on the wall, the figure of the fish managed to crawl onto three paintings simultaneously. The unrecognized masterpieces did not suffer from this, it must be admitted.

But a special place on the wall of Romolo's restaurant is occupied by a light-blue Italian national team jersey with the autographs of the players. The blue icon is sandwiched between two thick sheets of transparent plastic, each about a centimeter thick.

I don't know if the restaurant owner is aware of the incident at the National Gallery in London when activists from some (can't remember which) movement splashed tomato soup on Van Gogh's painting. Judging by everything, he is.

Unlike Van Gogh's painting, the football icon is unlikely to be worth £73 million. At least, not now. But Romolo clearly hopes that someday it will.

—

Chapter 25

Fabrizio

My grandfather had an old folding pocket knife that he always carried in his pocket. Just in case it might come in handy.

I can't say he really used it often, but my grandfather was a practical man, and this nice habit of carrying a folding knife suited him. Sometimes, he would let me take a look at it. I remember that knife as if it were yesterday: a worn wooden handle with a dark patina from time, and a blade with a matte metallic sheen.

The knife also had a small, slightly rusty bottle opener. With great pride and a loud "sh-sh-sh-pop," I would open the lemonade that my grandfather often bought for me.

An amazing thing.

You might wonder, what does Italy have to do with my grandfather's old folding knife? Allow me to explain.

I have a "geometra," and his name is Fabrizio. I got to know him through connections, just like my accountant Simona, my landlord, my dentist, and everyone else on the list. You remember how it works.

So, a "geometra" is a person you need if you want to buy property, build something, do renovations, and so on. He understands technical matters and knows how to coordinate all these actions with the local municipality. In short, a Handy Man.

Fabrizio lives in a new district of the city, completely devoid of historical heritage. Yes, maybe there is heritage there, but it's buried deep underground. When something is being built in Italy, sooner or later, the excavator's bucket will come across an Etruscan settlement, or Roman baths, or early Christian catacombs. Nevertheless, this historical heritage is not visible from the outside.

It seemed to me that Fabrizio wasn't very fond of it. He reasoned simply: construction would be halted, archaeologists would arrive, and they would spend a long time digging in the pit with small shovels and eagerly cleaning clay fragments with brushes.

When Fabrizio came to assess the technical condition of the Italian apartments I was planning to buy in the historic part of the city (remember those 26 square meters with the Moroccan guy inside?), my "geometra" was extremely concise:

— Problema, — said Fabrizio.

We continued the inspection of the apartments, and everything that "geometra" said after that either started with the word "problema" or ended with the word "problema."

Yes, the word "problema" was indeed appropriate in many cases. Yes, old Italy has seen better days. Yes, the houses in the historic part of the city were built centuries ago, and the condition of the electrical and plumbing systems is the least resembling a dream for Fabrizio. That's true.

But I suddenly realized that my pragmatic "geometra" doesn't see any charm in the cracks on the stone masonry of centuries-old walls, which I love to admire. For him, uneven cobblestone, carefully laid (as far as the ancients could) by the order of Emperor Augustus, holds no value. All the mentioned above is nothing more than a "problema" for Fabrizio.

And the Etruscan arch definitely needs thorough restoration. It's been standing for three thousand years; it's about time.

I think if Fabrizio became a senator, he would propose updating the ancient stucco and finally painting the remnants of the Colosseum in a nice beige color. After that, he would announce a national tender to equip the amphitheater with sturdy plastic windows. Double-glazed, with an air chamber — to prevent drafts.

Yes, often Italy does look worn, sometimes even too much so, but I can't imagine it any other way; I don't want to see it restored. Just like my grandfather's old folding pocket knife. It's a pity that it got lost somewhere, and I haven't been able to find it. Although I would really like to.

And it's good that Fabrizio is not a Roman senator but my "geometra."

—

Chapter 26

The Man with the Big Knife

In Umbria, they bake unsalted bread. A type of bread I had never bought before. Then, little by little, I began to understand its purpose, but it took a long time for comprehension to settle in — about a year.

Unsalted bread is one of the few Italian products that I found challenging to get used to. Although, in general, I love Italian bread, with the exception of "pane sciapo"— that Umbrian bread. It is baked entirely without salt.

Once, I asked the seller at the local "panetteria" (bread shop) — a big guy with a huge knife in his hands — to tell me why this bread is unsalted and who on earth needs it.

As a result, I was treated to a fairly extensive culinary-historical lecture with patriotic undertones:

"Since various types of salami that we produce and consume in considerable quantities have a very rich taste, they need a neutral accompaniment, a sidekick. Something that won't overpower the flavor of the best salami in Italy. Ours, that is. That's why here, in Umbria, we started baking unsalted bread 'pane sciapo,' and we, tough Umbrians, are damn proud of it."

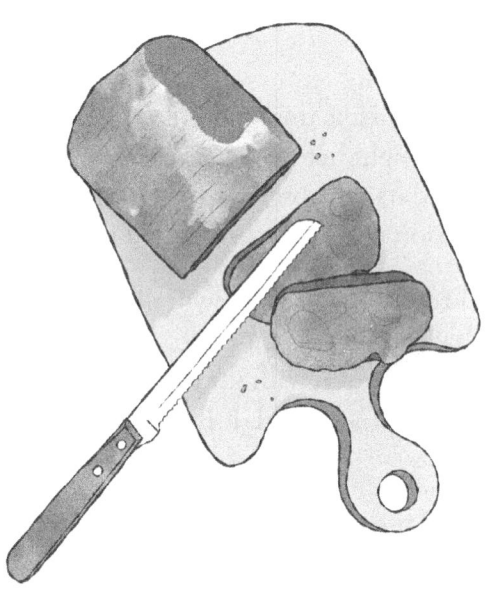

In general, an acute sense of patriotism is definitely characteristic of Italians. But it's not as straightforward as one might think. The patriotism of Italians doesn't look the way you might imagine. Italians themselves joke that they become Italians only during the World Cup. And who are they when there is no World Cup?

They are Umbrians, Tuscans, Ligurians, Sicilians, and so on down the list. They are not Italians. Each of them has their own unsalted bread of global significance, the world's best olive oil, or some dish made from chicken innards that is undoubtedly worthy of UNESCO's World Heritage status.

Each of them will talk for hours about the bluest sea, unparalleled in nature, the incredible beauty of the mountains, and the best people you won't find anywhere else but in the region of Italy where they were born. And it's delightful.

A Neapolitan will never become a Milanese. Yes, they may move from Naples to Milan, and many have actually done so.

Southern Italy has never been known for, and still isn't known for, rapid industrial development. It is not a financial center of the world, Europe, or even Italy itself. Therefore, the problem of unemployment has always existed in the south. Young southerners saw no prospects for their future and moved north. In reality, they still continue to do so, although not on the same scale as in the post-war period. The process has slowed down, but it hasn't stopped.

Neapolitans, Sicilians, Calabrians move to Milan, Turin, and Bologna, but they don't become Milanese, Turinese, or Bolognese. They remain Neapolitans, Sicilians, Calabrians.

They carefully carry their little homeland in their hearts, not exchanging it for anything. They preserve grandma's recipes and sing lullabies to their children in Neapolitan, Sicilian, and Calabrian. They admit that their little homelands have problems, poverty, and unemployment. Many of them have the same mafia, after all. But they become Italians only during the World Cup.

By the way, for the sake of fairness, it should be noted that unsalted bread is baked not only in Umbria. But I chose not to voice this inconvenient information.

—

Chapter 27

Fabio, Mirco & Gabriele

My friend Fabio called me:

— Do you have a compass?

— You might be surprised, but no.

— Damn it, get ready, we're going to the mountains.

— Where?

— To the mountains!

— Uh-uh-uh... But we are already in the mountains, we live here.

— No-no-no, to the real mountains.

Fabio found an announcement somewhere about a sports orienteering tournament and for some reason decided that we absolutely had to participate. Keep in mind that he had done it only once before, and I had never done it.

But this fact proved insufficient to stop this crazy idea, and we decided to go. Due to our lack of experience, both of us, without consulting each other, made the rather foolish decision to wear shorts. Something I quickly realized when I saw other tournament participants in outfits resembling scuba diving gear.

For about three hours, we raced through rugged terrain with maps in hand, searching for orange flags. People in scuba suits occasionally whizzed past us. But overall, I enjoyed it. Except for the scratches on my legs due to the shorts blunder.

Fabio is not an athlete in general. He works as a milling machine operator somewhere on the outskirts of the city. But he also dances the Tarantella — he takes dance lessons. Besides, he's always ready for something else. And he's not an exception.

Little Mirco's car comes to my house every day at 5:40 PM. He comes to pick up the trash. It's a different type of trash every day: organic, plastic and metal, paper, glass, and "indifferenziato"— for cases when it's not very clear which category the waste belongs to.

I went down and handed Mirco a bag of garbage. Yellow, it seems. Which means it contains plastic and metal. Mirco responds:

— Oh, I forgot to give you my business card. Wait a bit. Don't leave yet.

 I stand, waiting. Meanwhile, Mirco energetically rummages through the glove compartment to find his business card. So energetically that the little car sways in all directions under the weight of its not-so-young driver.

— There it is! Here it is! Take it.

That's how I found out that the man who picks up my trash every day at exactly 5:40 PM doesn't just do that. He organizes trips to interesting places in Umbria. For free. Just to show them to people.

About a year ago, I also met a guy who sells used books a hundred meters from my house. Mostly, these are albums with works by Renaissance artists—he says they sell the best. I even bought some book from him. Now, though, I don't remember exactly what.

And only a year later, I learned that the seller of albums with Botticelli, Raphael, and Da Vinci's masterpieces also makes documentary films. He doesn't get paid for them, but he likes it. The seller's name is Gabriele.

It seems Italians, somehow, have learned not to limit themselves to one profession or one occupation. Many of those I know easily and very naturally combine several roles within themselves. And they try new ones.

Of course, it's not because they are descendants of the brilliant Da Vinci, whose albums are popular in Gabriele's store. But I have no other theories.

—

Chapter 28

Maurizio

Rome is the first city in Italy that I saw with my own eyes. I saw it, and that was it: love at first sight. Genuine love.

However, I don't always recognize it now. It has changed. Not over three thousand years. In the last twenty years. The preceding three thousand years were more stable than the past few decades. I often come back here. I guess I miss it.

I stand on a small narrow street, and about a hundred meters ahead is the amazing Roman square — Piazza Navona. Those who have been there with me, I think, will agree. I don't know how many times I've been there: 300, 400, 500? Definitely a lot.

Right above me is a small balcony. I know for sure that it can fit one small round table, a folding chair, and exactly one person of slender build. Just like me twenty years ago.

To get to this small balcony, you need to enter the wooden door — it's right underneath it. Then you need to go up the narrow spiral staircase, trying not to hit the iron knight who stands right at its steepest turn.

It's important not to hit him because the knight is very expensive to its owner — Maurizio, who gets quite upset when the iron head of the knight once again rolls down the stairs with a crash. And when Maurizio gets upset, he threatens to fire everyone to hell, as he is not only the owner of the iron knight but also the owner of this establishment (it's a pub), as well as the small balcony that we've been climbing to for so long. He has the right to do so, although he sometimes goes overboard with strong language.

I worked for Maurizio as a waiter twenty years ago when I was a student, and Maurizio also threatened to fire me a couple of times. But for some reason, he didn't.

Maurizio never let a single skirt pass by, and besides women, little else interested him. He didn't possess outstanding looks or charm. Maurizio was short, with a round belly and funny mustaches that everyone suggested he shave off. Some hinted, some spoke directly. None of the methods worked; Maurizio didn't want to part with his funny mustaches.

So, the women Maurizio was interested in showed absolutely no reciprocity. Although he had a lot of determination, attempts to pick up usually ended in failure. Maurizio's unsuccessful attempts to charm another Roman tourist were very amusing to all the employees of his pub, including me. For which Maurizio also threatened to fire me.

It is believed that Italians cherish traditions and treat cuisine with reverence. Many do. But since Maurizio was only interested in women, he was absolutely unconcerned about the prestige and centuries-old traditions of Italian cuisine. His establishment offered diluted alcohol and food of very questionable quality to tired tourists.

Despite being a pub, during lunch, you could eat pizza or a plate of pasta. Neither one could be called real Italian cuisine. Maurizio bought the pasta in paper plates, which were heated in the microwave. After that, the pasta from the paper plate proudly moved to a large white dish, as if it were a Michelin-starred restaurant, and was sent to the table of the next tourist. The tourist clearly made a mistake in choosing a place for lunch, but as long as he didn't know about it.

The same thing happened with the pizza: it was bought frozen and simply reheated. Once, a customer lifted the pizza on his plate and discovered a paper label stuck to the bottom. There was a big scandal, which didn't impress Maurizio at all, and he continued to do the same.

The balcony (the same one that fits exactly one skinny person, like me twenty years ago) is not for pub customers — it's for its own. Small, cozy, albeit a bit cramped. I came to see it. Specifically, to this balcony — it is especially dear to me.

The pub is no longer here; unfamiliar people are doing repairs, and from the street, you can hear someone inside lazily scraping off the expensive plaster that is dear to my heart.

What happened to Maurizio is also unknown.

—

Chapter 29

Valentina

From time to time, my iPhone pulls out old photos from the far corners of its memory and compiles photo albums from them. So, completely by accident, I found this photo. It shows only a coffee cup. A regular coffee cup made of white porcelain.

This cup earned its kilobytes in my phone not thanks to the correct foam that every self-respecting "espresso" should have. And not because in this photo, taken from above, my legs comically stick out from under the cup. It's not about that, although, indeed, my legs sticking out are quite amusing.

I often don't carry cash with me — it's summer, light clothing, nowhere to put a wallet.

I came for breakfast; Valentina handed me a pistachio "cornetto" and a cappuccino. I must say that now, when I come to the bar where Valentina works, we will definitely exchange a few phrases, discuss the news, or complain together about the cool weather. At that moment when I took this photo of the coffee cup, we didn't know each other.

So, with cappuccino and pistachio cornetto done, it's time to go home. I approached the cash register, tapped my card. It doesn't work. Tapped it again. Still doesn't work. The third time. Again, nothing. In general, it doesn't work at all, some malfunction at the bank, the app doesn't even open. It doesn't work, and there's no cash.

"Oh, well, forget about it, you can bring the money later. If you want, tomorrow," says Valentina.

I wasn't too upset about it and generally understood that it wasn't such a big problem. But I consider it important to maintain fragile cosmic balance, so I didn't even think about not returning the money. On the contrary, I usually try to do it quickly and fear forgetting because it would be awkward. That's my fixation — about the world, goodness, and all that.

In general, I went home, took cash, returned to the bar. And inside, the smell of coffee is so tempting that it's hard to resist. I decided to take an espresso as well – after all, I'm a customer with money now.

I finished the espresso, thanked Valentina for her understanding, repaid the debt. Valentina, in turn, thanked me for coming back. And flatly refused to take money for the espresso — as if I endured the inconvenience, not her.

The cup in the photo is that same cup. The one I didn't pay for. Which, I think, is worth not just one euro and twenty cents, as indicated in the bar's menu. At least five. Or ten. Maybe even more.

—

Chapter 30

Marco

Marco teaches Italian, loves to read, and writes books. He is 39 years old and lives with his father in the Apulian city of Bari in southern Italy. More precisely, he comes here for the summer. The rest of the year, he works abroad and criticizes the Italian financial, health-care, and tax systems from there.

Not forgetting to mention the pension system. It used to be there, but now it's not. Well, it is, of course, but not like before. And many other things are not like before. Almost everything is not like before.

My father does the same. He fondly remembers the lemonade that used to be sold exclusively in glass bottles, not plastic. Dad recalls the ice cream made from pure milk, and he also tenderly loves his drill, which was not made in China. Occasionally, he has to buy new drill bits for it. He says they're not the right ones. Not at all.

Marco and my father are very similar despite the age difference.

Marco loves to talk about the mint-colored Vespa scooter, on which, in the Italy he remembers, you could ride without a license. He remembers the tiny Fiat 500 car, magically fitting who knows how many people. And no one felt crowded.

I've never ridden a Fiat 500 and haven't even sat inside. But as for old Italian scooters like Vespa, they definitely have some inexplicable charm. Not the most rational one, but it's there.

In reality, they are not very comfortable — often downright uncomfortable. They are not as fast as modern ones, not as fuel-efficient, and "not the same" in many other ways.

But someone parked this beauty - Vespa, a hundred meters from my house, and now I just can't pass by: beautiful lines, stylish reddish-brown leather, and a round chrome mirror on a slender elegant stalk.

Although, if I'm completely honest, it's not even leather — it's synthetic. But even this inconvenient fact does not spoil the impression — still absolute beauty.

From time to time, Marco takes out a heavy Olivetti typewriter from the closet. It's inconvenient to type on it, although it's entirely possible. But even he admits that the MacBook is more convenient.

In general, it's a very Italian trait — to praise Italy of the past and criticize Italy of the present. Not only Marco does this.

Those who are older remember Italy in the 50s, 60s when there was an economic boom in the country, and it seemed that happiness would last forever.

They remember the San Remo Festival:

— That's where real music was. There! Not what it is now.

That's what they say.

Those who are a bit younger regret the early 2000s when Italy abandoned the lira and adopted the euro. Because of this, according to them, prices for everything doubled exactly. And until that moment, everything was good, and nothing needed to be changed.

But it's not about money. Marco doesn't want to earn all the money in the world. He doesn't want to earn at all. As, indeed, work. If it were possible, Marco would spend all 12 months in his port city — reading books and going in the evenings to watch the sea.

Perhaps, I would stay too. I like this place — simple, without unnecessary frills. Oysters are served right in the port on disposable plastic plates, and local fishermen enthusiastically slap octopuses onto the concrete dock, rinse sea urchins in blue basins, and drink icy beer at eight in the morning.

From Italy with love.

From the author:

I hope you enjoyed this book. I've put all my heart and soul into it, so that you can feel the atmosphere of Italy and come to love its people too.

Since I'm self-publishing this book, without the help of publishing houses or producers, I would greatly appreciate it if you could leave a review. You would make me truly happy by writing a few words or adding a photo of the book.

It won't take more than two minutes:

1. Point your smartphone camera at the QR code below

2. Write me a few words about the book

Thank you in advance!
Sincerely yours, Sergio Néster

Thank you for reading!

Printed in Great Britain
by Amazon